THIRTY VIRTUES

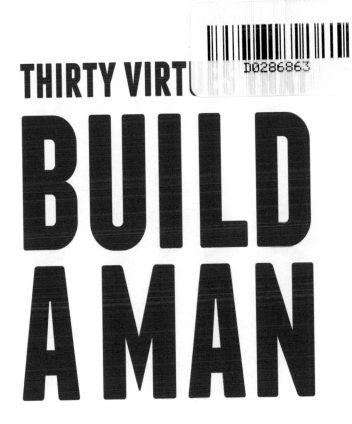

BUILD
A MAN

Vince Miller's books and materials for men are needed more than ever today because men are confused. In a world that has marginalized biblical masculinity; Thirty Virtues That Build a Man *is a brilliant solution. Each chapter is concise, biblical, and practical. It's the perfect tool for any mentor, protégé, or man who wants to live as the best version of himself in Christ.*

Jim Ramos
Founder of The Great Hunt for God and Man Card Podcast

Vince Miller is passionate about seeing men follow Jesus with all they've got and has written a book that will help them do just that! Thirty Virtues That Build a Man *engages the reader with its easy-to-read format and then helps them apply the truths to their lives.*

Tom Henderson
Speaker, Author and Founder of Restoration Generation

Every man needs a mentor. And every mentor knows the power of great questions. Vince Miller has created a terrific resource to help the men you mentor live more intentionally.

Leary Gates
Venture Coach & Founder, BoldPath Life Strategies

Today, more than ever, men need focus and structure. Vince Miller, who has been encouraging men for over 20 years to grow in their faith, has given us just than in his new book Thirty Virtues That Build a Man. *It is designed to be used solo or even more effectively as a mentoring guide in thirty 2-page lessons. That's the structure. The focus is on thirty virtues every man needs to integrate into his heart and mind. This is a tool every father, husband or grandfather can use to encourage and build up younger men. It is a blueprint for discipling and mentorship, just what those of us who want to be used to build up others have been waiting for.*

Michael Card
Singer/Songwriter, Author, & Speaker

I'm grateful to recommend Thirty Virtues That Build a Man *as a tool for any man serious about transformational living. Vince's book will foster meaningful conversations amongst men who desire personal growth for Kingdom impact. The church needs more men who are willing to be vulnerable with one another so we can live lives that matter for all of eternity. This book is one tangible way we can make that happen.*

Jamie Miller
President, Consumed Ministries

Vince Miller understands the challenges men face in today's demanding society. In his newest book, Thirty Virtues That Build a Man. *Vince gives fresh, clear, actionable solutions that can bring freedom, a new start and lasting results. This book is a game changer!*

Ken Larson
President, Slumberland Furniture

Vince Miller's commitment and ministry to men is clear, passionate and unwavering. He has a calling that is undeniable and has a purpose for serving men. His content is incredible, and his delivery is authentic. He understands that all men need accountability and mentoring to be successful as husbands, fathers, grandfathers and as friends. Vince has my utmost respect and my committed prayers.

John Deedrick
Managing Director, Fourth Element Capital

The "Thirty" resources are exactly what men need today. Straight-forward, biblically-based, easy-to-use tools for men to use in private reflection or in mentoring. Using these resources, men will be challenged and equipped to experience the transforming power of Christ.

Dan Busby
President, Evangelical Christian Financial Association

THIRTY VIRTUES THAT
BUILD
A MAN

A CONVERSATIONAL GUIDE
FOR MENTORING ANY MAN

VINCE MILLER

Equip Press
Colorado Springs, Colorado

THIRTY VIRTUES THAT
BUILD A MAN
A Conversational Guide
for Mentoring Any Man

First Edition: 2018
Thirty Virtues That Build a Man: A Conversational Guide for Mentoring Any Man /
      Vince Miller
Paperback 978-1-946453-31-0
eBook ISBN: 978-1-946453-36-5

TO: _____

FROM: _____

NOTE: _____

_____

_____

_____

_____

_____

TABLE OF CONTENTS

A NOTE FROM THE AUTHOR

I pray this experience will benefit your life and your spiritual growth as a man. I hope you will do three things as you engage. First, I pray that you will be receptive to the Word of God. I love that in Resolute, we dig into the Bible every time we meet. The Bible is not an ordinary book; it is the means of discovering God and spiritual transformation, but it requires a receptive man. Second, lean into brotherhood by inviting another man to join you for *Thirty Virtues That Build a Man*. Build a friendship, share transparently, and have conversations that go beyond the superficial and shallow conversations we have every day. Third, put into action what you have learned. Choose an action item each week, knowing that one small step weekly leads to success over a lifetime.

Keep moving forward,

ABOUT RESOLUTE

WE DISCIPLE & DEVELOP MEN TO LEAD

We believe men are a strategic audience and force for change in the world and that God ordained men with power, authority, and the opportunity to define the world around them. While the culture would attempt to silence the voice of men by attacking their masculinity, exaggerating male short-comings, and belittling their Christian worldview, we believe this is not the answer. The answer is to build better men. When we build better men, we build better homes, marriages, workplaces, and churches. When one man gets better, everyone gets better.

But we have an enemy.

The enemy is not the culture, opposing beliefs, media, politics, or even pornography. The enemy is apathy. It is the appeal of inaction that lies within a man's heart. At Resolute, we have discovered, after leading thousands of men through mentoring, that the only thing that stands between us and a new brotherhood of men is a single man and his willingness to defy the impulse of apathy. It is the silent voice that entices him to say nothing and do nothing when God has called him to action.

At Resolute, we provide men with easy-to-use tools that help them fight the impulse of apathy. Here are a few.

1. **ON YOUR OWN | THE MEN'S DAILY DEVOTIONAL** is our tool for getting men into the Bible daily. It is free to use and share. You can find it at www.beresolute/mdd.

2. **ONE ON ONE |** *THIRTY VIRTUES THAT BUILD A MAN* is our tool for helping men build a brotherhood with the Bible. You can use it on your own, but it's always better to use with another man. You can use it again and again. You can find it at www.beresolute.org/thirty.

3. **IN A GROUP | MEN'S GROUP CONTENT** is for leading a group of men. There is no faster way to grow in your faith than to lead a group of men using small group videos for leaders and handbooks for partici-pants. www.beresolute.org/videos.

Visit **www.beresolute.org** to view the full content available.

USING THIRTY VIRTUES THAT BUILD A MAN

THE PURPOSE

This 30-lesson guide is for men to use in private reflection or conversations with other men. It is written to invite character development conversations for men of any age, as well as spiritual development, and can be used repeatedly.

THE PROCESS

1 | BUILD YOURSELF

Read through one virtue each week and answer the questions within the lesson. Each lesson uses our B.U.I.L.D. process.

- **BEGIN** with the goal.
- **UNPACK** your thoughts.
- **INFORM** through the Bible.
- **LAND** on action steps.
- **DO** one action for one week.

2 | BROTHER UP

Take each lesson further by partnering up with another man. Use the 30 lessons as a mentoring and discipleship tool that takes all the guesswork out of a spiritual conversation. Brother up with a friend, neighbor, church member, associate, or relative.

THE PAYOFF

If you stay with the process for all 30 lessons, you will grow in character as a man of God. Often, men just need a plan to get moving spiritually. This book is a plan—a method and a process that results in outcomes with a rich spiritual payoff.

RECEPTIVITY

begin

A man of God is receptive to God's truth over a lifetime.

unpack

What is the one task you had to do last week that you were unreceptive to doing?

What about the task, or you, made it objectionable?

inform

Read the text and make observations.

How many soils are in the text?

What are the characteristics of each?

What does the "soil" represent?

4 And when a great crowd was gathering and people from town after town came to him, he said in a parable, **5** "A sower went out to sow his seed. And as he sowed, some fell along the path and was trampled underfoot, and the birds of the air devoured it. **6** And some fell on the rock, and as it grew up, it withered away, because it had no moisture. **7** And some fell among thorns, and the thorns grew up with it and choked it. **8** And some fell into good soil and grew and yielded a hundredfold." As he said these things, he called out, "He who has ears to hear, let him hear." **9** And when his disciples asked him what this parable meant, **10** he said, "To you it has been given to know the secrets of the kingdom of God, but for others they are in parables, so that 'seeing they may not see, and hearing they may not understand.' **11** Now the parable is this: The seed is the word of God. **12** The ones along the path are those who have heard; then the devil comes and takes away the word from their hearts, so that they may not believe and be saved. **13** And the ones on the rock are those who, when they hear the word, receive it with joy. But these have no root; they believe for a while, and in time of testing fall away. **14** And as for what fell among the thorns, they are those who hear, but as they go on their way they are choked by the cares and riches and pleasures of life, and their fruit does not mature. **15** As for that in the good soil, they are those who, hearing the word, hold it fast in an honest and good heart, and bear fruit with patience.

LUKE 8:4–15

land

Which soil do you represent? One or many? In what areas are you more receptive to the truth?

What issues do you need to address?

What steps do you need to take?

do

Ask someone to evaluate your receptivity.

ACTION

A Man Fights Apathy

begin

A man of God fights apathy with action.

unpack

As a kid, what was one of the dumbest things you did?

What are the most prevalent sins you see taking down men in the home, work, or in churches today? Why?

What impact do these sins have on culture, business, families, and the church?

inform

Read the text and make observations.

What was the serpent's method of temptation?

What was woman's temptation?

What was man's temptation?

What was woman's response after sin?

What was man's response after sin?

[1] Now the serpent was more crafty than any other beast of the field that the Lord God had made. He said to the woman, "Did God actually say, 'You shall not eat of any tree in the garden'?" [2] And the woman said to the serpent, "We may eat of the fruit of the trees in the garden, [3] but God said, 'You shall not eat of the fruit of the tree that is in the midst of the garden, neither shall you touch it, lest you die.'" [4] But the serpent said to the woman, "You will not surely die. [5] For God knows that when you eat of it your eyes will be opened, and you will be like God, knowing good and evil." [6] So when the woman saw that the tree was good for food, and that it was a delight to the eyes, and that the tree was to be desired to make one wise, she took of its fruit and ate, and she also gave some to her husband who was with her, and he ate. [7] Then the eyes of both were opened, and they knew that they were naked. And they sewed fig leaves together and made themselves loincloths. [8] And they heard the sound of the Lord God walking in the garden in the cool of the day, and the man and his wife hid themselves from the presence of the Lord God among the trees of the garden. [9] But the Lord God called to the man and said to him, "Where are you?" [10] And he said, "I heard the sound of you in the garden, and I was afraid, because I was naked, and I hid myself." [11] He said, "Who told you that you were naked? Have you eaten of the tree of which I commanded you not to eat?" [12] The man said, "The woman whom you gave to be with me, she gave me fruit of the tree, and I ate." [13] Then the Lord God said to the woman, "What is this that you have done?" The woman said, "The serpent deceived me, and I ate."

GENESIS 3:1–13

land

Where do you need to take action in your life?
What steps do you need to take?

do

Decide one action step and do it.

PRAYER

A Man Speaks Up

begin

A man of God talks to the God he loves.

unpack

What is your prayer pattern? (For example: how often do you pray, what do you typically pray about, what time of day do you pray?)

If you could change anything about your prayer patterns, what would you change?

inform

Read the text and make observations.

What did Jesus teach his men was the right motive for prayer?

From your reading of the Lord's Prayer, what are essential topics of a Christ-like prayer. List them.

5 "And when you pray, you must not be like the hypocrites. For they love to stand and pray in the synagogues and at the street corners, that they may be seen by others. Truly, I say to you, they have received their reward. 6 But when you pray, go into your room and shut the door and pray to your Father who is in secret. And your Father who sees in secret will reward you. 7 "And when you pray, do not heap up empty phrases as the Gentiles do, for they think that they will be heard for their many words. 8 Do not be like them, for your Father knows what you need before you ask him. 9 Pray then like this: "Our Father in heaven, hallowed be your name. 10 Your kingdom come, your will be done, on earth as it is in heaven. 11 Give us this day our daily bread, 12 and forgive us our debts, as we also have forgiven our debtors. 13 And lead us not into temptation but deliver us from evil. 14 For if you forgive others their trespasses, your heavenly Father will also forgive you, 15 but if you do not forgive others their trespasses, neither will your Father forgive your trespasses."

MATTHEW 6:5–15

land

What are the most significant prayers you have ever prayed and the most significant answers you have ever received?

What would you ask for prayer about right now in your life?

do

Deploy the A.C.T.S. method of prayer. (Adoration, Confession, Thanksgiving, and Supplication.)

FAITH

A Man Muscles Up

begin

A man battles human fear with a reverent fear.

unpack

Over the last few weeks, what themes or issues consumed your mental energy? Describe the situations. What about these situations generated human fear?

inform

Over the last few weeks, what themes or issues consumed your mental energy? Describe the situations. What about these situations generated human fear?

22 Immediately he made the disciples get into the boat and go before him to the other side, while he dismissed the crowds. 23 And after he had dismissed the crowds, he went up on the mountain by himself to pray. When evening came, he was there alone, 24 but the boat by this time was a long way from the land, beaten by the waves, for the wind was against them. 25 And in the fourth watch of the night he came to them, walking on the sea. 26 But when the disciples saw him walking on the sea, they were terrified, and said, "It is a ghost!" and they cried out in fear. 27 But immediately Jesus spoke to them, saying, "Take heart; it is I. Do not be afraid." 28 And Peter answered him, "Lord, if it is you, command me to come to you on the water." 29 He said, "Come." So Peter got out of the boat and walked on the water and came to Jesus. 30 But when he saw the wind, he was afraid, and beginning to sink he cried out, "Lord, save me." 31 Jesus immediately reached out his hand and took hold of him, saying to him, "O you of little faith, why did you doubt?" 32 And when they got into the boat, the wind ceased. 33 And those in the boat worshiped him, saying, "Truly you are the Son of God."

MATTHEW 14:22–33

land

In what area do you sense Jesus inviting you to step out in faith?

What human fears do you need to address?

What steps do you need to take?

do

Identify and act on a faith decision today.

REPENTANCE

When Man Makes a Change

begin

God's man feels the full responsibility of sin and then makes a change without looking back.

unpack

Identify one behavior you would like to change in someone you know. Explain how the undesirable behavior impacts you.

Can you recall the last time you heard a politician say, "I'm sorry"? Why is admitting failure or changing behavior so difficult?

inform

Read the text and make observations.

Why do you think repent is the first word Jesus ever preached about in Matthew 4:17?

What is the promise for repentant people in 2 Chronicles 7:14?

What factors are involved in repentance for the younger brother in Luke 15:17–19? How do you think this young man would define repentance?

17 "From that time Jesus began to preach, saying, 'Repent, for the kingdom of heaven is at hand.'"

MATTHEW 4:17

14 "If my people who are called by my name humble themselves and pray and seek my face and turn from their wicked ways, then I will hear from heaven and will forgive their sin and heal their land."

2 CHRONICLES 7:14

17 "But when he came to himself, he said, 'How many of my father's hired servants have more than enough bread, but I perish here with hunger! **18** I will arise and go to my father, and I will say to him, "Father, I have sinned against heaven and before you. **19** I am no longer worthy to be called your son. Treat me as one of your hired servants."'"

LUKE 15:17–19

land

What have been the hardest thoughts, behaviors, or attitudes for you to change or repent of?

What do you need to repent of today? Consider whether your repentance is an issue of awareness, sorrow, action, or motivation.

What steps do you need take to embrace repentance?

do

Take steps of repentance today.

BELIEFS

Belief Determines Man's Direction

begin

A man's beliefs determine his direction.

unpack

What corrupted belief do you see in society? Why do you believe people fall for this corrupted belief? (Consider the areas of business, politics, education, religion, finance, etc.)

How have you blown it lately? Consider the negative behavior and the emotion that went with this failure.

Now share the "corrupt belief" that was driving this behavior or emotion.

inform

Read the text and make observations.

What mindsets do you find in the text?

What is the focus of these mindsets?

What is the result of these mindsets?

[5] For those who live according to the flesh set their minds on the things of the flesh, but those who live according to the Spirit set their minds on the things of the Spirit. [6] For to set the mind on the flesh is death, but to set the mind on the Spirit is life and peace. [7] For the mind that is set on the flesh is hostile to God, for it does not submit to God's law; indeed, it cannot. [8] Those who are in the flesh cannot please God.

ROMANS 8:5–8

 land

What percentage of the time is your mindset set on things of the flesh versus things of the Spirit?

What issues do you need to address to increase your mindset of the Spirit?

What steps can you take?

do

Remove distractions and build a spiritual mindset.

IDENTITY

The Definition of Man

begin

God's man finds his identity in what God says about him.

unpack

What is the most spectacular experience you have had in life?

What about you changed after this experience?

What do you think of yourself as God's man on most days? Try to be open and honest.

inform

Read the text and make observations.

How many times does Paul use the word "in"?

What attributes do we find "in Christ" or "in him?"

How does this text strengthen you?

[1] Paul, an apostle of Christ Jesus by the will of God, to the saints who are in Ephesus, and are faithful in Christ Jesus: [2] Grace to you and peace from God our Father and the Lord Jesus Christ. [3] Blessed be the God and Father of our Lord Jesus Christ, who has blessed us in Christ with every spiritual blessing in the heavenly places, [4] even as he chose us in him before the foundation of the world, that we should be holy and blameless before him. In love [5] he predestined us for adoption as sons through Jesus Christ, according to the purpose of his will, [6] to the praise of his glorious grace, with which he has blessed us in the Beloved. [7] In him we have redemption through his blood, the forgiveness of our trespasses, according to the riches of his grace, [8] which he lavished upon us, in all wisdom and insight [9] making known to us the mystery of his will, according to his purpose, which he set forth in Christ [10] as a plan for the fullness of time, to unite all things in him, things in heaven and things on earth. [11] In him we have obtained an inheritance, having been predestined according to the purpose of him who works all things according to the counsel of his will, [12] so that we who were the first to hope in Christ might be to the praise of his glory. [13] In him you also, when you heard the word of truth, the gospel of your salvation, and believed in him, were sealed with the promised Holy Spirit, [14] who is the guarantee of our inheritance until we acquire possession of it, to the praise of his glory.

EPHESIANS 1:1–14

land

Do you think about yourself as Paul describes man in this text?

What issues do you need to address to realize your identity like Paul does in Ephesians 1?

What steps do you need to take?

do

View your identity today in Christ.

RENEWING

The Mindset of a Better Man

begin

A man must renew his mindset every day because he lives in a rapidly changing world.

unpack

As you were growing up, was there ever a significant transformation you experienced physically, mentally, or emotionally? What was this like?

What is one of the most transformational insights you have gained to this point in life?

List the most damaging thoughts that people have about God that keep them from believing in God?

inform

Read the text and make observations.

How would you define the word "conformed?"

How would you define the word "transformed?"

How would you define the word "renewal?"

Why do you think Paul includes "humble thinking" as part of the process of renewing the mind?

[1] I appeal to you therefore, brothers, by the mercies of God, to present your bodies as a living sacrifice, holy and acceptable to God, which is your spiritual worship. [2] Do not be conformed to this world, but be transformed by the renewal of your mind, that by testing you may discern what is the will of God, what is good and acceptable and perfect. [3] For by the grace given to me I say to everyone among you not to think of himself more highly than he ought to think, but to think with sober judgment, each according to the measure of faith that God has assigned.

ROMANS 12:1–3

inform

Read the text and make observations.

How would you define the word "conformed?"

How would you define the word "transformed?"

How would you define the word "renewal?"

Why do you think Paul includes "humble thinking" as part of the process of renewing the mind?

do

Renew your mind in one area.

KNOWING

A Man Welcomes Intimacy

begin

God's man welcomes an intimate relationship with God and others.

unpack

What prominent leader, living or dead, would you love to meet?

If you were invited to eat at a significant event featuring this leader, what would be your initial response?

How would your view of this leader change if he invited you to dine with him privately and he opened up to you his personal challenges?

inform

Read the text and make observations.

Thomas uses a different Greek word for the verb "to know" than Jesus uses. We cannot see this in our English text. Thomas' word for "to know" in verse 5 infers "propositional knowledge." Jesus' word for "to know" in verse 9 infers a "personal knowledge." With this understanding, how does the text read differently?

What can you conclude from this understanding?

[5] Thomas said to him, "Lord, we do not know where you are going. How can we know the way?" [6] Jesus said to him, "I am the way, and the truth, and the life. No one comes to the Father except through me. [7] If you had known me, you would have known my Father also. From now on you do know him and have seen him." [8] Philip said to him, "Lord, show us the Father, and it is enough for us." [9] Jesus said to him, "Have I been with you so long, and you still do not know me, Philip? Whoever has seen me has seen the Father. How can you say, 'Show us the Father'? [10] Do you not believe that I am in the Father and the Father is in me? The words that I say to you I do not speak on my own authority, but the Father who dwells in me does his works. [11] Believe me that I am in the Father and the Father is in me, or else believe on account of the works themselves.

JOHN 14:5–11

land

Of the three types of knowledge (**propositional** — "knowing that"; **process** — "knowing how"; and **personal** — "knowing by acquaintance"), where do you spend most of your time "knowing" God?

What steps can you take to know God more intimately?

do

Engage in a discipline that will help you know God more intimately. Choose one of the following: **praying**, **silence**, **reading**, **generosity**, or **service**.

UNDERSTANDING

The Enlightened Man

begin

A man enlightened by Jesus acts in contrast to the world.

unpack

What is one critical learning that has been enlightening for you in your family of origin, marriage, work, or church?

How has this learning has impacted your life?

inform

Read the three texts and make observations.

What does the word "light" represent in the texts?

What does the word "darkness" represent?

What is the assumed tool, or tools, for "illuminating?"

5 "This is the message we have heard from him and proclaim to you, that God is light, and in him is no darkness at all. **6** If we say we have fellowship with him while we walk in darkness, we lie and do not practice the truth. **7** But if we walk in the light, as he is in the light, we have fellowship with one another, and the blood of Jesus his son cleanses us from all sin. **8** If we say we have no sin, we deceive ourselves, and the truth is not in us. **9** If we confess our sins, he is faithful and just to forgive us our sins and to cleanse us from all unrighteousness. **10** If we say we have not sinned, we make him a liar, and his word is not in us.

1 JOHN 1:5–10

105 "Thy word is a lamp unto my feet, and a light unto my path."

PSALM 119:105

12 "Again Jesus spoke to them, saying, 'I am the light of the world. Whoever follows me will not walk in darkness, but will have the light of life.'"

JOHN 8:12

land

Where do you need cleansing, the Word, and light in your life as man?
What steps can you take to confess your darkness?

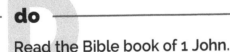

do

Read the Bible book of 1 John.

SUBMISSION

The Position of Man

begin

A man is someone who can submit to authority, knowing that he needs to be governed.

unpack

What are reasons men run from authority? List three.

What are the blessings of authority? List three.

Is there ever a time we should not submit to authority? Be specific.

inform

Read the text and make observations.

What disturbs you about this text?

God created authority and government to govern people. Three of these institutions are government, church, and family/marriage. Why did God create them based on Romans 13:1–7?

How are we to respond to these?

[1] Let every person be subject to the governing authorities. For there is no authority except from God, and those that exist have been instituted by God. [2] Therefore whoever resists the authorities resists what God has appointed, and those who resist will incur judgment. [3] For rulers are not a terror to good conduct, but to bad. Would you have no fear of the one who is in authority? Then do what is good, and you will receive his approval, [4] for he is God's servant for your good. But if you do wrong, be afraid, for he does not bear the sword in vain. For he is the servant of God, an avenger who carries out God's wrath on the wrongdoer. [5] Therefore one must be in subjection, not only to avoid God's wrath but also for the sake of conscience. [6] For because of this you also pay taxes, for the authorities are ministers of God, attending to this very thing. [7] Pay to all what is owed to them: taxes to whom taxes are owed, revenue to whom revenue is owed, respect to whom respect is owed, honor to whom honor is owed.

ROMANS 13:1–7

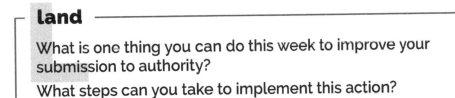

land

What is one thing you can do this week to improve your submission to authority?

What steps can you take to implement this action?

do

Pray for your government officials and church leaders.

SACRIFICE

A Man Is a Giver

begin

A man is willing to make hard sacrifices and does not take but gives.

unpack

Why were sacrifices offered in the Old Testament?

When is the last time someone sacrificed for you?

How do you think God would define sacrifice?

inform

Read the text and make observations.

How many times does Jesus say "cannot?"

Jesus requires the crowd to give up their family of origin for his mission. What would make this challenging for this crowd of followers?

What does the building parallel teach us?

What does the battle parallel teach us?

25 Large crowds were traveling with Jesus, and turning to them he said: **26** "If anyone comes to me and does not hate father and mother, wife and children, brothers and sisters—yes, even their own life—such a person cannot be my disciple. **27** And whoever does not carry their cross and follow me cannot be my disciple. **28** "Suppose one of you wants to build a tower. Won't you first sit down and estimate the cost to see if you have enough money to complete it? **29** For if you lay the foundation and are not able to finish it, everyone who sees it will ridicule you, **30** saying, 'This person began to build and wasn't able to finish.' **31** "Or suppose a king is about to go to war against another king. Won't he first sit down and consider whether he is able with ten thousand men to oppose the one coming against him with twenty thousand? **32** If he is not able, he will send a delegation while the other is still a long way off and will ask for terms of peace. **33** In the same way, those of you who do not give up everything you have cannot be my disciples. **34** "Salt is good, but if it loses its saltiness, how can it be made salty again? **35** It is fit neither for the soil nor for the manure pile; it is thrown out. "Whoever has ears to hear, let them hear."

LUKE 14:25–35

land

What issues do you need to address, and what steps do you need to take to increase your willingness to sacrifice?

do

Sacrifice some of your time for a friend.

OBEDIENCE

A Man Is Compliant to God

begin

A man is radically compliant to God, knowing that obedience must be learned.

unpack

Think about a person in your family of origin or extended family who is known for their disobedience. Take a moment to describe what they do and how their actions impact others.

In culture, what defines obedience and disobedience? What are the complications of culture defining morality? How does this need to be addressed?

What are the consequences of disobedience?

What are the rewards of obedience?

inform

Read the text and make observations.

What are the two gates and their characteristics?

What do you believe the "gate" represents?

What do the "characteristics" of the gates represent?

inform (continued)

In verses 15–23 we are warned to beware. Of who, what, and why are we to beware?

What are the fruits of obedience?

---

[13] "Enter by the narrow gate. For the gate is wide and the way is easy that leads to destruction, and those who enter by it are many. [14] For the gate is narrow and the way is hard that leads to life, and those who find it are few. [15] Beware of false prophets, who come to you in sheep's clothing but inwardly are ravenous wolves. [16] You will recognize them by their fruits. Are grapes gathered from thorn bushes, or figs from thistles? [17] So, every healthy tree bears good fruit, but the diseased tree bears bad fruit. [18] A healthy tree cannot bear bad fruit, nor can a diseased tree bear good fruit. [19] Every tree that does not bear good fruit is cut down and thrown into the fire. [20] Thus you will recognize them by their fruits. [21] "Not everyone who says to me, 'Lord, Lord,' will enter the kingdom of heaven, but the one who does the will of my Father who is in heaven. [22] On that day many will say to me, 'Lord, Lord, did we not prophesy in your name, and cast out demons in your name, and do many mighty works in your name?' [23] And then will I declare to them, 'I never knew you; depart from me, you workers of lawlessness.'

MATTHEW 7:15–23

land

What voices do you need to eliminate to become more obedient to God?

What steps do you need to eliminate these voices?

do

When God prompts your heart, obey quickly.

SELF-DISCIPLINE

The Practice of a Man

begin

A man welcomes and practices self-discipline as a means of diminishing the desires of the flesh.

unpack

Define self-discipline in your own words.

What keeps men from living with self-discipline?

List spiritual disciplines that a Christian man can use to build self-discipline. How do these spiritual disciplines build self-discipline?

inform

Read the text and make observations.

Paul imagines two athletic events in the early "Olympic" games. What are the events?

What spiritual lesson is Paul teaching using these two events?

What does "strict training" look like in a man's life? Describe in detail what you think Paul was addressing.

24 Do you not know that in a race all the runners run, but only one gets the prize? Run in such a way as to get the prize. **25** Everyone who competes in the games goes into strict training. They do it to get a crown that will not last, but we do it to get a crown that will last forever. **26** Therefore I do not run like someone running aimlessly; I do not fight like a boxer beating the air. **27** No, I strike a blow to my body and make it my slave so that after I have preached to others, I myself will not be disqualified for the prize.

1 CORINTHIANS 9:24–27

land

Name one spiritual discipline you would like to build?

Walk through the steps below and reflect how you can build this discipline.

1. **CHOOSE** a discipline.
2. **SCHEDULE** the discipline.
3. **ACT** on the discipline.
4. **TWEAK** the discipline.
5. **REPEAT** the process.

do

Focus on one spiritual discipline and build self-discipline.

PURPOSE

The Reason Behind a Man

begin

God's man may look for purpose in possessions and professions, but he only finds real purpose in Jesus Christ.

unpack

Of the 3.5 billion men on earth, what percentage both know their purpose and live it? Make your best guess.

Why do you believe men struggle to find purpose?

What is the purpose of your business?

What is the purpose of your role within this company?

Does the connection between company purpose and your role result in purposefulness? Explain.

inform

Read the text and make observations.

Why did God's people spend 70 years of captivity in Babylon?

What is God's promise to them through this experience?

inform *(continued)*

What does God require of them in and through this captivity?

What is the outcome on the other side of captivity?

What lesson is God hoping the people will learn?

[10] For thus says the Lord: When seventy years are completed for Babylon, I will visit you, and I will fulfill to you my promise and bring you back to this place. [11] For I know the plans I have for you, declares the Lord, plans for welfare and not for evil, to give you a future and a hope. [12] Then you will call upon me and come and pray to me, and I will hear you. [13] You will seek me and find me, when you seek me with all your heart. [14] I will be found by you, declares the Lord, and I will restore your fortunes and gather you from all the nations and all the places where I have driven you, declares the Lord, and I will bring you back to the place from which I sent you into exile.

JEREMIAH 29:10–14

land

What lesson is God trying to teach you currently about His purpose in your life?

How would your life be more productive if you aligned your purpose with his purpose?

do

Align your vocational purpose to God's purpose by working in a manner that honors God.

PRODUCES

A Man Yields Growth

begin

A man never selfishly devours resources but instead understands that resources flow from Christ through him.

unpack

Do you feel like you are producing results in your spiritual life?

What are the leading issue(s) that prohibit you from producing more spiritual results.

inform

Read the text and make observations.

What vital activity is Jesus recommending for producing growth, and what does it look like for a man to be effective at this?

What are we invited to abide in, and what are the promised results?

How well do you currently abide?

[1] "I am the true vine, and my Father is the vinedresser. [2] Every branch in me that does not bear fruit he takes away, and every branch that does bear fruit he prunes, that it may bear more fruit. [3] Already you are clean because of the word that I have spoken to you. [4] Abide in me, and I in you. As the branch cannot bear fruit by itself, unless it abides in the vine, neither can you, unless you abide in me. [5] I am the vine; you are the branches. Whoever abides in me and I in him, he it is that bears much fruit, for apart from me you can do nothing. [6] If anyone does not abide in me he is thrown away like a branch and withers; and the branches are gathered, thrown into the fire, and burned. [7] If you abide in me, and my words abide in you, ask whatever you wish, and it will be done for you. [8] By this my Father is glorified, that you bear much fruit and so prove to be my disciples."

JOHN 15:1–8

land

What issue, or issues, are impeding your growth and production?

What steps can you take to address this?

do

Memorize one verse from John 15:1–8 and abide in it. You can also take the Spiritual Fruit Assessment here: **www.beresolute.org/sfa**.

MOTIVE

The Force Behind a Man

begin

God's man is aware that his motives will be influenced by forces that attempt to satisfy his desires.

unpack

Is it right to judge the motives of another person?

How do you tell when a person is purely motivated?

How do know when your motives are pure?

inform

Read the text and make observations.

What is a hypocrite?

Why do hypocrites sound trumpets in the streets?

How does this "sounding your trumpet" relate to "practicing your righteousness?"

How does giving in secret expose our true motive?

[1] "Beware of practicing your righteousness before other people in order to be seen by them, for then you will have no reward from your Father who is in heaven. [2] "Thus, when you give to the needy, sound no trumpet before you, as the hypocrites do in the synagogues and in the streets, that they may be praised by others. Truly, I say to you, they have received their reward. [3] But when you give to the needy, do not let your left hand know what your right hand is doing, [4] so that your giving may be in secret. And your Father who sees in secret will reward you."

MATTHEW 6:1–4

land

Why do you need to monitor your motives?
What steps do you need to take?

do

Check your motive by performing an anonymous act of generosity for another man.

BROTHERHOOD

A Man Is Devoted to His Brothers

begin

A man of God, while enticed by autonomy, must live out his quest by linking arms with his brothers.

unpack

Why do we spend so little time with other Christian brothers?

Make a short list of reasons men need other brothers in Christ?

inform

Read the text and make observations.

Why does Jesus pray for our oneness?

Jesus gives us an example of the oneness between him and God. Describe the characteristic of this oneness.

What does "oneness" or "brotherhood" look like for men of God?

20 "I do not ask for these only, but also for those who will believe in me through their word, **21** that they may all be one, just as you, Father, are in me, and I in you, that they also may be in us, so that the world may believe that you have sent me. **22** The glory that you have given me I have given to them, that they may be one even as we are one, **23** I in them and you in me, that they may become perfectly one, so that the world may know that you sent me and loved them even as you loved me."

JOHN 17:20–23

land

What are the results of men living in brotherhood?

How would these results have a positive impact your life?

Who is a Christian man with whom you would like to spend more time?

do

This week, give another man a copy of *Thirty Virtues That Build a Man* and build brotherhood.

CORE BELIEFS

Man Leads from What He Believes

begin

God's man leads from his core beliefs, which guide how he thinks, feels, and acts.

unpack

Discuss in detail a recent event that created some frustration or anxiety for you. It could be a tiny issue; for example, something you watched on the news or something that happened at work.

What were your thoughts about the event? Make sure to list them.

What do you think these thoughts say about your beliefs? Clarify if needed.

Discuss where you think you picked up this belief and whether this belief impacts other areas of your thinking.

inform

Read the text and make observations.

Why does God care so much about idols?

What represents a "god" in today's culture

inform *(continued)*

What is the punishment for bowing down and serving these gods?

In contrast, what is the reward for worshipping God?

[1] And God spoke all these words, saying, [2] "I am the Lord your God, who brought you out of the land of Egypt, out of the house of slavery. [3] You shall have no other gods before me. [4] "You shall not make for yourself a carved image, or any likeness of anything that is in heaven above, or that is in the earth beneath, or that is in the water under the earth. [5] You shall not bow down to them or serve them, for I the Lord your God am a jealous God, visiting the iniquity of the fathers on the children to the third and the fourth generation of those who hate me, [6] but showing steadfast love to thousands of those who love me and keep my commandments.

EXODUS 20:1–6

land

What is one core belief that you picked up as a child? This belief might have been stated as an axiom and could be either positive or negative. Discuss how this impacted your beliefs then and today. (For example, "Big boys don't cry." "Man-up." "Stop being a baby."

Is it surprising to discover that core beliefs you are not aware of may infuence your life? How should a Christian man address this?

do

Make God the center of everything you do.

VALUES

The Measure of Every Man

begin

A man of God is driven by the things he values.

unpack

It's the middle of the night, and there is a fire in your home. If you could save only one item, what would you choose? Explain your choice. (Assume your family and pets are already safely out of harm's way.)

What value compelled you to choose this item?

Think about your family of origin. What value do you hold that is different from your family of origin? Explain.

inform

Read the text and make observations.

Notice the comparison between "lips" and "heart." What does this comparison infer?

What do you think "wonder upon wonder" means?

What is troubling about this text?

13 And the Lord said: "Because this people draw near with their mouth and honor me with their lips, while their hearts are far from me, and their fear of me is a commandment taught by men, **14** therefore, behold, I will again do wonderful things with this people, with wonder upon wonder; and the wisdom of their wise men shall perish, and the discernment of their discerning men shall be hidden." **15** Ah, you who hide deep from the Lord your counsel, whose deeds are in the dark, and who say, "Who sees us? Who knows us?"

ISAIAH 29:13–15

land

Write out your top personal values? Consider nouns like faith, teamwork, discipline, and generosity. Name five that hold deep meaning for you.

Describe each of your five values in detail in your own words. Give them any definition you like.

How can you live up to these values?

do

Discuss one of your values with someone.

VISION

A Man's Sight

begin

God's man leads others with vision.

unpack

Describe your relationship with your father growing up by reflecting on a story about him.

How did your father parent you? Think about his methodology and try to describe it.

What principles did he live by in his fathering technique? What best practices were helpful for you as a child?

Tell your group partner why it's vital for you to be a great parent.

inform

Read the text and make observations.

David is casting a vision for Solomon, his son. What is his statement of vision?

What is required of Solomon to complete the vision?

How often do you think David thought about the vision he gave to Solomon?

⁹ "And you, Solomon my son, know the God of your father and serve him with a whole heart and with a willing mind, for the Lord searches all hearts and understands every plan and thought. If you seek him, he will be found by you, but if you forsake him, he will cast you off forever. ¹⁰ Be careful now, for the Lord has chosen you to build a house for the sanctuary; be strong and do it."

²⁰ Then David said to Solomon his son, "Be strong and courageous and do it. Do not be afraid and do not be dismayed, for the Lord God, even my God, is with you. He will not leave you or forsake you, until all the work for the service of the house of the Lord is finished. ²¹ And behold the divisions of the priests and the Levites for all the service of the house of God; and with you in all the work will be every willing man who has skill for any kind of service; also the officers and all the people will be wholly at your command."

1 CHRONICLES 28:9–10, 20–21

land

A vision is a picture of the future. It addresses some problem and provides a solution. What vision has God given you for your life? Write it out in 10 words or less.

do

Share your vision with someone.

MISSION

What a Man Does with Vision

begin

A man of God lives out his vision with a mission statement.

unpack

Imagine working in a business situation where your supervisor was unclear about your job duties. Why would this be frustrating?

Think of someone you know who has an apparent personal mission. What are the unseen benefits of how this person lives?

inform

Read the text and make observations.

Jonah was given a mission directly from God. Most men dream of this moment. Speculate about why Jonah ran from his God-given mission?

What does your conclusion teach us about the convergence of God's mission and our mission?

[18] Where there is no prophetic vision the people cast off restraint but blessed is he who keeps the law.

PROVERBS 29:18

[1] Now the word of the Lord came to Jonah the son of Amittai, saying, [2] "Arise, go to Nineveh, that great city, and call out against it, for their evil has come up before me." [3] But Jonah rose to flee to Tarshish from the presence of the Lord. He went down to Joppa and found a ship going to Tarshish.

JONAH 1:1–3

land

Do you feel like you live in God's mission? Why or why not?

What issues do you need to address?

What steps can you take today?

do

Write out God's mission for your life. (Hint: Consider your God-given gifts and talents and the context in which they best fit.)

GOALS

The Aim of a Man

begin

God's man sets goals; otherwise, he aims and hits nothing.

unpack

Why do people avoid setting goals?
Why are goals good for our spiritual life?

inform

Read the text and make observations.
What are the strengths of Nehemiah's approach?
What are the weaknesses of Nehemiah's approach?
What are the opportunities for Nehemiah?
What are the threats for Nehemiah?
What goals did Nehemiah set in this text?

[1] In the month of Nisan, in the twentieth year of King Artaxerxes, when wine was before him, I took up the wine and gave it to the king. Now I had not been sad in his presence. [2] And the king said to me, "Why is your face sad, seeing you are not sick? This is nothing but sadness of the heart." Then I was very much afraid. [3] I said to the king, "Let the king live forever! Why should not my face be sad, when the city, the place of my fathers' graves, lies in ruins, and its gates have been destroyed by fire?" [4] Then the king said to me, "What are you requesting?" So I prayed to the God of heaven. [5] And I said to the king, "If it pleases the king, and if your servant has found favor in your sight, that you send me to Judah, to the city of my fathers' graves, that I may rebuild it." [6] And the king said to me (the queen sitting beside him), "How long will you be gone, and when will you return?" So it pleased the king to send me when I had given him a time. [7] And I said to the king, "If it pleases the king, let letters be given me to the governors of the province Beyond the River, that they may let me pass through until I come to Judah, [8] and a letter to Asaph, the keeper of the king's forest, that he may give me timber to make beams for the gates of the fortress of the temple, and for the wall of the city, and for the house that I shall occupy." And the king granted me what I asked, for the good hand of my God was upon me.

NEHEMIAH 2:1–8

land

What goals do you need to set in your life?

do

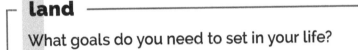

Set one spiritual goal and do it. Take this assessment for next time: **www.beresolute.org/sga**.

SPIRITUAL GIFTS

How God Equips a Man

begin

A man of God uses his God-given gifts not for his benefit, but for the benefit of others.

unpack

If money was no object and you could do anything you wanted the rest of your life, what would you spend it doing?

Try our Spiritual Gifts Assessment online at **www.beresolute.org/sga**.

inform

Read the text and make observations.

What does it mean to be a "living sacrifice"?

What does it mean to be a "member" of the body?

How are our gifts used to help one another in the body?

[1] I appeal to you therefore, brothers, by the mercies of God, to present your bodies as a living sacrifice, holy and acceptable to God, which is your spiritual worship. [2] Do not be conformed to this world, but be transformed by the renewal of your mind, that by testing you may discern what is the will of God, what is good and acceptable and perfect. [3] For by the grace given to me I say to everyone among you not to think of himself more highly than he ought to think, but to think with sober judgment, each according to the measure of faith that God has assigned. [4] For as in one body we have many members, and the members do not all have the same function, [5] so we, though many, are one body in Christ, and individually members one of another. [6] Having gifts that differ according to the grace given to us, let us use them: if prophecy, in proportion to our faith; [7] if service, in our serving; the one who teaches, in his teaching; [8] the one who exhorts, in his exhortation; the one who contributes, in generosity; the one who leads, with zeal; the one who does acts of mercy, with cheerfulness.

ROMANS 12:1–8

land

Based on your spiritual gifts assessment, what were your top 3–5 spiritual gifts?

Which gift scored lowest?

Was this assessment accurate for you?

How do your gifts fit into the body of Christ?

do

Use your top spiritual gift.

FEEDBACK

A Man Knows His Blind Spots

begin

God's man is receptive to feedback and invites it from others.

unpack

Think of someone you know who is entirely unreceptive to feedback. Discuss why this person is unreceptive to receiving feedback.

What is the purpose of feedback? For the giver? For the receiver?

When is the last time you invited personal feedback?

inform

Read the text and make observations.

Does Zedekiah appear open to feedback?

Consider what Jeremiah is risking by giving Zedekiah feedback?

What is the promise made by Zedekiah? Why do you think Zedekiah has to make this promise?

20 Listen to advice and accept instruction, that you may gain wisdom in the future.

PROVERBS 19:20

14 King Zedekiah sent for Jeremiah the prophet and received him at the third entrance of the temple of the Lord. The king said to Jeremiah, "I will ask you a question; hide nothing from me." **15** Jeremiah said to Zedekiah, "If I tell you, will you not surely put me to death? And if I give you counsel, you will not listen to me." **16** Then King Zedekiah swore secretly to Jeremiah, "As the Lord lives, who made our souls, I will not put you to death or deliver you into the hand of these men who seek your life."

JEREMIAH 38:14–16

land

How can you become more receptive to feedback?

If you became more receptive, what results would this produce?

do

Ask someone you trust for feedback. Use the feedback tool here: **www.beresolute.org/rsa**.

TRUST

A Man's Greatest Asset

begin

A man greatest asset in leadership is the trust he builds with those who follow him.

unpack

Have you ever worked for a supervisor who micro-managed? How did this feel?

List five activities of a leader that build trust.

What is the relationship between trust and vulnerability?

Can you trust someone you fear?

inform

Read the text and make observations.

How does the Lord build trust with Joshua?

What is required of Joshua to learn if he can trust God?

What is the promise made to Joshua for trusting in God?

How are trust and faith related?

[1] After the death of Moses the servant of the Lord, the Lord said to Joshua the son of Nun, Moses' assistant, [2] "Moses my servant is dead. Now therefore arise, go over this Jordan, you and all this people, into the land that I am giving to them, to the people of Israel. [3] Every place that the sole of your foot will tread upon I have given to you, just as I promised to Moses. [4] From the wilderness and this Lebanon as far as the great river, the river Euphrates, all the land of the Hittites to the Great Sea toward the going down of the sun shall be your territory. [5] No man shall be able to stand before you all the days of your life. Just as I was with Moses, so I will be with you. I will not leave you or forsake you. [6] Be strong and courageous, for you shall cause this people to inherit the land that I swore to their fathers to give them. [7] Only be strong and very courageous, being careful to do according to all the law that Moses my servant commanded you. Do not turn from it to the right hand or to the left, that you may have good success wherever you go. [8] This Book of the Law shall not depart from your mouth, but you shall meditate on it day and night, so that you may be careful to do according to all that is written in it. For then you will make your way prosperous, and then you will have good success. [9] Have I not commanded you? Be strong and courageous. Do not be frightened, and do not be dismayed, for the Lord your God is with you wherever you go."

JOSHUA 1:1–9

land

Which factor contributes most to those you place your trust in: their skill, how they care, or the integrity with which they do things?

How can you use skill, care, and integrity to build trust with those you lead or those who follow you?

do

Do what you say you will do and build trust.

MARGIN

A Man's Load and Limits

begin

God's man is always aware of the space between his load and his limits, and he manages this margin.

unpack

Share what an ideal, weekly schedule would look like?

Would you be more useful as a disciple and leader if you had a more balanced schedule? Why?

inform

Read the text and make observations.

What are the disciples' hope when they find their desolate place?

What is the contrast in the response of Jesus versus the disciples? Why the different reactions?

How does Jesus interact with people when their demands dictate a response from him?

Even though they are all tired, Jesus appears calm and centered. Why do you think this is?

[30] The apostles returned to Jesus and told him all that they had done and taught. [31] And he said to them, "Come away by yourselves to a desolate place and rest a while." For many were coming and going, and they had no leisure even to eat. [32] And they went away in the boat to a desolate place by themselves. [33] Now many saw them going and recognized them, and they ran there on foot from all the towns and got there ahead of them. [34] When he went ashore he saw a great crowd, and he had compassion on them, because they were like sheep without a shepherd. And he began to teach them many things. [35] And when it grew late, his disciples came to him and said, "This is a desolate place, and the hour is now late. [36] Send them away to go into the surrounding countryside and villages and buy themselves something to eat." [37] But he answered them, "You give them something to eat." And they said to him, "Shall we go and buy two hundred denarii worth of bread and give it to them to eat?" [38] And he said to them, "How many loaves do you have? Go and see." And when they had found out, they said, "Five, and two fish." [39] Then he commanded them all to sit down in groups on the green grass. [40] So they sat down in groups, by hundreds and by fifties. [41] And taking the five loaves and the two fish he looked up to heaven and said a blessing and broke the loaves and gave them to the disciples to set before the people. And he divided the two fish among them all. [42] And they all ate and were satisfied. [43] And they took up twelve baskets full of broken pieces and of the fish. [44] And those who ate the loaves were five thousand men.

MARK 6:30–44

land

What issues, demands, beliefs, or imposed values keep you from implementing a more balanced schedule?
What steps do you need to take?

do

Make space in your week for five minutes of personal devotions each day. Try the Men's Daily Devotional on the Resolute website: **www.beresolute.org/mdd**.

CHANGE

A Man Anticipates Change

begin

God's man understands that God does not change; therefore, he must.

unpack

What is the most significant change you have been through in your life, and what made this change hard? (Be as specific and as transparent as possible.)

When you hear these statements at work, what do they mean?
- "That is not the way we do things around here."
- "It is what it is."
- "It's not my job."

inform

Read the text and make observations.

What change is happening in the text, and why is this hard for both men?

What change does Saul experience?

What change does Ananias experience?

What are the risks for each man?

3 Now as he went on his way, he approached Damascus, and suddenly a light from heaven shone around him. **4** And falling to the ground he heard a voice saying to him, "Saul, Saul, why are you persecuting me?" **5** And he said, "Who are you, Lord?" And he said, "I am Jesus, whom you are persecuting. **6** But rise and enter the city, and you will be told what you are to do." **7** The men who were traveling with him stood speechless, hearing the voice but seeing no one. **8** Saul rose from the ground, and although his eyes were opened, he saw nothing. So they led him by the hand and brought him into Damascus. **9** And for three days he was without sight, and neither ate nor drank. **10** Now there was a disciple at Damascus named Ananias. The Lord said to him in a vision, "Ananias." And he said, "Here I am, Lord." **11** And the Lord said to him, "Rise and go to the street called Straight, and at the house of Judas look for a man of Tarsus named Saul, for behold, he is praying, **12** and he has seen in a vision a man named Ananias come in and lay his hands on him so that he might regain his sight." **13** But Ananias answered, "Lord, I have heard from many about this man, how much evil he has done to your saints at Jerusalem. **14** And here he has authority from the chief priests to bind all who call on your name." **15** But the Lord said to him, "Go, for he is a chosen instrument of mine to carry my name before the Gentiles and kings and the children of Israel. **16** For I will show him how much he must suffer for the sake of my name." **17** So Ananias departed and entered the house. And laying his hands on him he said, "Brother Saul, the Lord Jesus who appeared to you on the road by which you came has sent me so that you may regain your sight and be filled with the Holy Spirit." **18** And immediately something like scales fell from his eyes, and he regained his sight. Then he rose and was baptized; **19** and taking food, he was strengthened.

ACTS 9:3–19

land

What change needs to happen in your life today?
What steps do you need to take?

do

Make a change you have resisted.

CONFLICT

A Man Who Responds

begin

God's man knows how to respond to and manage conflict.

unpack

Share a time that you had to disagree with a rule or approach.

When you are confronted with an issue that catches you by surprise, what is your primary emotional response? How about your secondary response?

What tips or tricks help you deal with conflict when it arises? (For example: "I try to not immediately respond to an angry person.")

inform

Read the text and make observations.

What is the conflict management process suggested by Jesus?

How many steps are there in the process and what is the hope with each step taken?

15 "If your brother sins against you, go and tell him his fault, between you and him alone. If he listens to you, you have gained your brother. **16** But if he does not listen, take one or two others along with you, that every charge may be established by the evidence of two or three witnesses. **17** If he refuses to listen to them, tell it to the church. And if he refuses to listen even to the church, let him be to you as a Gentile and a tax collector. **18** Truly, I say to you, whatever you bind on earth shall be bound in heaven, and whatever you loose on earth shall be loosed in heaven. **19** Again I say to you, if two of you agree on earth about anything they ask, it will be done for them by my Father in heaven. **20** For where two or three are gathered in my name, there am I among them."

MATTHEW 18:15–20

land

What part of the conflict process is hardest for you? What steps do you need to take in the future during a conflict?

do

In your next conflict, thoughtfully respond.

DELEGATION

A Man's Team

begin

God's man is competent in his ability and can delegate to those around him.

unpack

Describe a situation where you have apprehension about delegating. Think about home or work.

There are many reasons we don't delegate. List them. Which of these reasons is the top 1–2 for you?

inform

Read the text and make observations.

What problem does Moses' father-in-law see in Moses' leadership process?

How does low self-awareness contribute to the problem for Moses?

What strategic change is recommended for Moses?

13 The next day Moses sat to judge the people, and the people stood around Moses from morning till evening. **14** When Moses' father-in-law saw all that he was doing for the people, he said, "What is this that you are doing for the people? Why do you sit alone, and all the people stand around you from morning till evening?" **15** And Moses said to his father-in-law, "Because the people come to me to inquire of God; **16** when they have a dispute, they come to me and I decide between one person and another, and I make them know the statutes of God and his laws." **17** Moses' father-in-law said to him, "What you are doing is not good. **18** You and the people with you will certainly wear yourselves out, for the thing is too heavy for you. You are not able to do it alone. **19** Now obey my voice; I will give you advice, and God be with you! You shall represent the people before God and bring their cases to God, **20** and you shall warn them about the statutes and the laws, and make them know the way in which they must walk and what they must do. **21** Moreover, look for able men from all the people, men who fear God, who are trustworthy and hate a bribe, and place such men over the people as chiefs of thousands, of hundreds, of fifties, and of tens. **22** And let them judge the people at all times. Every great matter they shall bring to you, but any small matter they shall decide themselves. So it will be easier for you, and they will bear the burden with you. **23** If you do this, God will direct you, you will be able to endure, and all this people also will go to their place in peace."

EXODUS 18:13–23

land

How does your knowledge of self and situations play into your ability and willingness to delegate?

What issues do you need to address, and what steps do you need to take?

do

Delegate one task to someone.

OUR NEXT BOOK IN THE THIRTY SERIES

THIRTY

MEN WHO LIVED WITH CONVICTION

Sample a lesson on the next page.

MOSES

The Master Mentor

begin

God's man understands that mentoring is not a choice but a mandate of following Christ.

unpack

Name an active or passive mentor (author, speaker) in your life?

What types of activities did they engage in mentoring you?

Have you ever formally mentored someone? If yes, describe what you did.

What keeps people from mentoring?

inform

Read the text and make observations.

What mentoring process is suggested here?

What activities are involved?

What is the skill required of the leader?

What is the time allocation?

4 "Hear, O Israel: The Lord our God, the Lord is one. **5** You shall love the Lord your God with all your heart and with all your soul and with all your might. **6** And these words that I command you today shall be on your heart. **7** You shall teach them diligently to your children, and shall talk of them when you sit in your house, and when you walk by the way, and when you lie down, and when you rise. **8** You shall bind them as a sign on your hand, and they shall be as frontlets between your eyes. **9** You shall write them on the doorposts of your house and on your gates.

DEUTERONOMY 6:4–9

land

What skills do you possess for mentoring someone?

What allocation of time can you give to mentoring someone?

How can you use this book to mentor someone you know?

do

Buy this book for another man, and either mentor them or encourage them to mentor someone else.

ABOUT THE AUTHOR

Vince Miller grew up on the West Coast and was born in Vallejo, California, where he spent his childhood. At age 20, he made a profession of faith, and while in college, he felt a call to work in full-time ministry. After college and graduate school, Vince invested two decades working with notable ministries like Young Life, Intervarsity Christian Fellowship, the local church, and in senior interim and teaching roles. He currently lives in St. Paul, Minnesota with Christina, his wife. They have three children—Faith, Grant, and Riley.

Vince is an authentic and transparent leader who loves to communicate to men and has a deep passion for God's Word. He has authored numerous books and small group guides for men, and he is the primary creator of all Resolute content and training materials.

See Vince's profile here:

www.beresolute.org/vince-miller

KEYNOTE SPEAKER TO MEN

Are you looking for a motivational and engaging communicator for your next men's retreat, conference, or event?

Engage men with a powerful message and inspire your men to action.

Like many young men, Vince Miller, born in the California, Bay Area, grew up without a father in the home. However, after his mother's second failed marriage, his grandfather took him in and mentored him into manhood. His compelling story of the problem and need for building better men has impassioned thousands of men to live with greater conviction and become the men God intended them to be. Prepare to be challenged with his message entitled, "Build Better Men."

To find out more or reach out to Vince Miller directly, go to our website. **www.beresolute.org/vince-miller**

DISTRIBUTE OR DONATE
THIRTY VIRTUES THAT BUILD A MAN

Are you looking for an easy way to support men who are searching for mentors or brotherhood in line with God's Word?

If you would like, you can purchase more copies of *Thirty Virtues That Build a Man* and distribute them to men in need. We are looking for donors to provide boxes of books to men living in halfway homes, prisons, and detox centers. We are also looking for supporters to help us distribute boxes to colleges, universities, and men serving in the armed forces. Just visit our website to gift a box of 60 or more books to men of your choosing or connect us to people who you feel can help.

www.beresolute.org/thirty

GROUP CONTENT FOR MEN

Are you looking for small group content for men?

Resolute has a growing library of video-led content that men across the country use for their existing men's small groups. Try one of our many popular multi-week studies. Begin with *Attributes for Men*, which leads a group in ten sessions through nine life-altering attributes modeled by the ultimate man, Jesus Christ.

Check out the trailer and material on the website.

www.beresolute.org/attributes-promo

THE MEN'S DAILY DEVO

Do you need a great daily devotional made just for men?

If you have not tapped into the Men's Daily Devotional, then you need to get it today. It consists of short, daily devotionals that you can use and share with other men. You can subscribe on the website.

www.beresolute.org/mdd

FINANCIAL SUPPORT

Are you looking for a great organization to support that believes in putting the Bible in the hands of men and promoting brotherhood?

Resolute is a 501(c)(3) non-profit organization. All gifts to our organization are tax deductible. Consider partnering with us so we can continue to put resources in the hands of men who cannot afford our tools and resources.

www.beresolute.org/donate

CPSIA information can be obtained
at www.ICGtesting.com
Printed in the USA
FSHW011530090419
57081FS